HOT SPOTS

33 Polka Dot Art Quilts

Eleanor Knowles Dugan

Grand Cyrus Press
San Francisco

© 2013 by Eleanor Knowles Dugan
All rights reserved
Printed in the United States of America

ISBN 978-0-9790994-7-2
Library of Congress Control Number: 2013930532

Dugan, Eleanor Knowles, 1937 —
Hot Spot: 33 Polka Dot Art Quilts

Design by Ann Marra

Photos by Sharon Risedorph, Dani Lawler, and Marlyse Fuller

For information, contact:

Grand Cyrus Press
1024 Sacramento Street
San Francisco, CA 94108-2003

www.GrandCyrusPress.com

To Freddy Moran

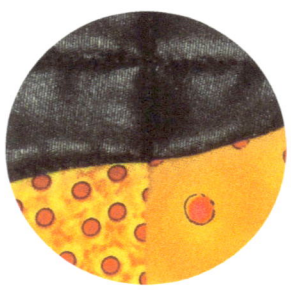

Contents

Preface	11
Introduction	15
The Block	17
The Fabric	20
33 Polka Dot Art Quilts	22
Low-Tech Dots	64
Embellishments	66
APPENDIX A: About the Block	67
APPENDIX B: Resources	68
APPENDIX C: My Life in Rags	69
Alphabetical List of Quilts	72
Biographies	73

Preface

I've always loved polka dots! They make me happy. Perhaps because they distill a graphic element signaling imminent fun, separated from the traditional clown character which is so often frightening to children.

Although my personal life has been devoted to political activism and community service for more than fifty years, my current art quilts have no social, political, or narrative messages. They seek simply to delight and intrigue, providing a few moments of pure pleasure. If these pieces can make people—however harried, weary, or distressed—break out in a big smile of surprise, I've succeeded. (There is entirely too much angst in the world!)

Acknowledgments

My thanks to Freddy Moran who originally inspired me and then encouraged me; to Mary Mashuta, in whose "Lotsa Dots" class I conceived the first dot quilt in my cycle; to Nancy Crow for insisting that quilts should always be made in a series, exploring an idea as far as it can go; to Dr. Seuss and his story, *The 500 Hats of Bartholomew Cubbins*, for giving me a goal; to Dani Lawler and Katrina Lamken who became part of the process when arthritis threatened to halt the journey; and to my daughter, Jill Coogan, who always sees the big picture.

Eleanor Knowles Dugan
San Francisco, 2013

Introduction

This is the story of a single polka dot that multiplied. The first dot quilt, humble #1, was begun in a 2001 workshop. That could and should have been the end of it. However, the dictum of quilt artist Nancy Crow is always to work in a series, expanding on a concept through at least three or four pieces to see how far you can take the initial idea. Stop when you've said everything you have to say. (See her quote below.)

At first it was hard to advance on this first quilt, a quilt that already said so much. Then ideas became a tumult, and soon I was rushing to finish each variation so I could try something else new. It became a journey.

Now, a dozen years and nearly three-dozen pieces later, I am still obsessed. Currently there are thirty-three polka dot quilts and counting.

> *[W]orking in a series is important because there's a tendency on the part of an artist to want to resolve everything in one piece. I think that's a grand mistake because it's biting off too much. Why not break it down and start at some point and do that piece, see what's wrong with it, go on to the next piece and resolve that area? At the same time, you're constantly making connections back and forth...as you go on, the whole thing gets richer and richer. That doesn't mean that when you see the whole series of, let's say, 20 pieces, that maybe number two was [one of the] best pieces.*
>
> Interview with Nancy Crow, Dec. 18, 2002,
> http://www.aaa.si.edu/collections/interviews/oral-history-interview-nancy-crow-13095

The Block

So you want to "push a block" as far as you can, but which block? There are hundreds, even thousands, to choose from. While you contemplate, here is the history of the block I chose and why I chose it. First, the original basic block.

Traditional 2-piece block

This block has several names including Borrow from Peter to Pay Paul or Rob Peter to Pay Paul. These names refer to the apparent construction method which is similar to Ponzi schemes, those fraudulent investment operations that pay investors with their own money or money from subsequent investors rather than from any profits. This block is sometimes erroneously called Drunkard's Path, which is actually a "set" of the block. (See below.)

A number of other blocks share these names because they look as if the fabric removed from one part of the block can be swapped out with the opposite piece from another to form two new blocks, each the reverse of the other. In fact, the missing seam allowance usually makes this impossible.

Sets

Any asymmetrical block can be rotated through four positions.

Statistically, laying an asymmetrical, two-color block on a large grid in different arrangements can create hundreds of thousands of possible arrangements—4 (blocks) to the power of the number of blocks. Adding a third color can produce millions of possibilities. The most artistic of grids using this block have become traditional patterns or "sets" and go by a variety of names: Drunkard's Path, Mill Wheel, Steeplechase, Wanderer of the Wilderness, Solomon's Puzzle, Old Maid's Puzzle, Old Maid's Dilemma, Jockey Cap, Rocky Road to Dublin, Fool's Puzzle, Wish-U-Well, Sunshine and Shadows, Falling Timbers and more. (Some of these names also describe quilts that use a completely different block.)

In 2001, I took a "Lotsa Dots" workshop with designer/author Mary Mashuta in Berkeley, California. She advised her students to bring a wide range of polka dot fabrics, and we were provided with her pattern for a variation of the traditional block.

Mary Mashuta offers her students a popular variation of the block that she calls "Circle within a Square."

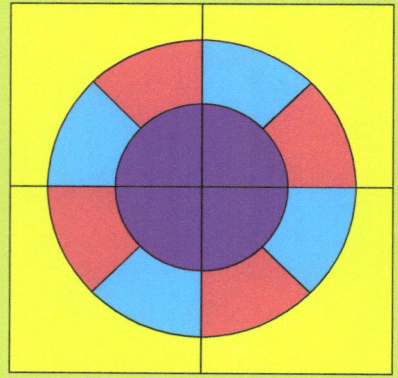

This pattern provides an exciting way to include four different fabrics in a small area, but the arc is positioned off center on the edge of the block, so that a continuous line can be created with only one setting—a circle.

While any other set causes a jazzy disconnect.

She encouraged her students to use both smooth and jazzy to create an interesting overall design

However, I wanted to be able to both circle and travel smoothly, so I redrafted her pattern, centering the ends of the arcs on the sides of the block.

My version of the block.

My block in circle set.

My block with the arc traveling.

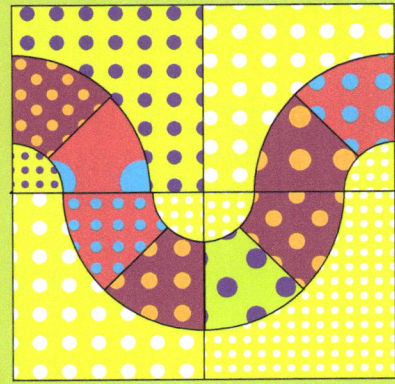

It is the traveling aspect of this block design that first captivated me. Other qualities struck me later.

The Fabric

To me, dots are dazzling points of light—stars in a night sky, sunlight dappling through leaves, sparkles on water. Fireworks. Chocolate chips. Fireflies. Trout leaping. Bubbles. Flickers of holiday lights reflected in excited, happy eyes.

Inspired by Freddy Moran's quilt "The Cow Jumped over the Stars," I had been collecting black-and-white dots for at least a decade, but I was unsure how I would use them.

Homage to Freddy's Cow I, 1996. 93˝ x 110˝.
By Eleanor Dugan

Many of my dots went into two homage quilts honoring Freddy Moran's vision, but I still had a huge stash of black-and-white polka dots.

33 Polka Dot Quilts

The "Lotsa Dots" workshop seemed the perfect opportunity to explore further. Mary Mashuta instructed her students to bring a wide range of dots in many colors, but my dot series was almost entirely black and white. With this limitation, I tried to create interest by having the backgrounds of the blocks morph into each other: black background with white dots becoming white background with black dots and vice versa.

My challenge to myself was to combine my minimal palette of fabrics into a coherent and merry whole. Ultimately, some of the fabrics had to be created with appliquéd dots, buttons, and embellishments, and I added a bit of color.

When the quilt was completed, the wooden balls seemed a natural extension, dots eager to tumble off the surface. I bought plain wooden balls, enlarged their holes with a drill so they were big enough to accommodate the thongs, and then painted them. I thought a knot at the end of each thong would securely hold the balls, but then a visiting child admired the piece and pulled one off. The balls are now firmly sewn in place with clear filament thread.

Hot Spot, 2001. 45˝ x 38˝, plus 6˝ fringe.

Next, I began wondering what I could do by combining primary colors with black, continuing use of the same Borrow from Peter block. I started with red and black. Happily, I found a few red-and-black dot fabrics in fabric stores and combined them with leftover black-and-white dot fabrics, overdyed red. Still, I needed more variety, so I designed 24 dot configurations on my computer, using Word. I printed them in black and white on paper and had these images converted to Thermofax silkscreens. Red dots were screened onto black fabrics and black dots were screened onto red fabrics, using opaque textile paints.

I planned to continue increasing the number of center holes in subsequent quilts for a *Ball Two* and *Ball Three*. I have not yet gone back to the theme of balls in holes in the larger pieces, though I've used it in some small quilts in a later series.

Ball One, 2003. 45˝ x 38˝, plus 8˝ fringe.

An innovative collection of contemporary French quilts at the Pacific International Quilt Festival in Santa Clara, California provided an "Aha!" moment, liberating me forever from conceiving of quilts as flat, rectangular, or uninterrupted. My arcing pathways began to escape the box more assertively.

Again, I did much overdyeing and silkscreening for *Sun Spot* to produce a wide range of yellow and black dots. I had planned to decorate this piece liberally with yellow and black wooden balls, but in the end decided that two would do.

Sun Spot, 2003. 45˝ x 38˝, plus 10˝ extension.

The final addition to the black-plus-color series was *Night Spot*.

Night Spot, 2003. 45˝ x 38˝, plus 5˝ fringe.

Dot-Dot-Dot was a small break-out study using primarily reject fabrics that I had tried to overdye red with Procion® dyes for *Ball One*. Due to some polyester content, they insisted on coming out a lucious 1940s DuBarry pink, dictating their destiny in a different quilt.

Dot-Dot-Dot, 2004. 27″ x 22″, including fringe.

While pondering where to go next, I folded my black-and-white fabrics into a storage bin. Then I began dividing my ever-growing stash of colored dots into color groups. As I handled and stroked the fabrics—tactility being one of the secret gratifications of quilting—the *Going Dotty* quilts automatically designed themselves. These quilts were the first to use entirely commercial fabrics.

Going Dotty I, 2004. 30˝ x 45˝, plus 16˝ extension.

Going Dotty II, 2004. 31˝ x 45˝, plus 11˝ extension.

After "going to black" (film term for the blackout between scenes) with primary colors, I wondered if I could morph two colors together. *Convergence One* was inspired by some commercial cerise-and-chartreuse dots designed by Jane Sassaman. Not a common color combination, so I created more cerise/chartreuse combos by buying cerise or chartreuse fabrics with white dots, then coloring the dots with fabric markers in the opposite color. Other dots were appliquéd or machine embroidered.

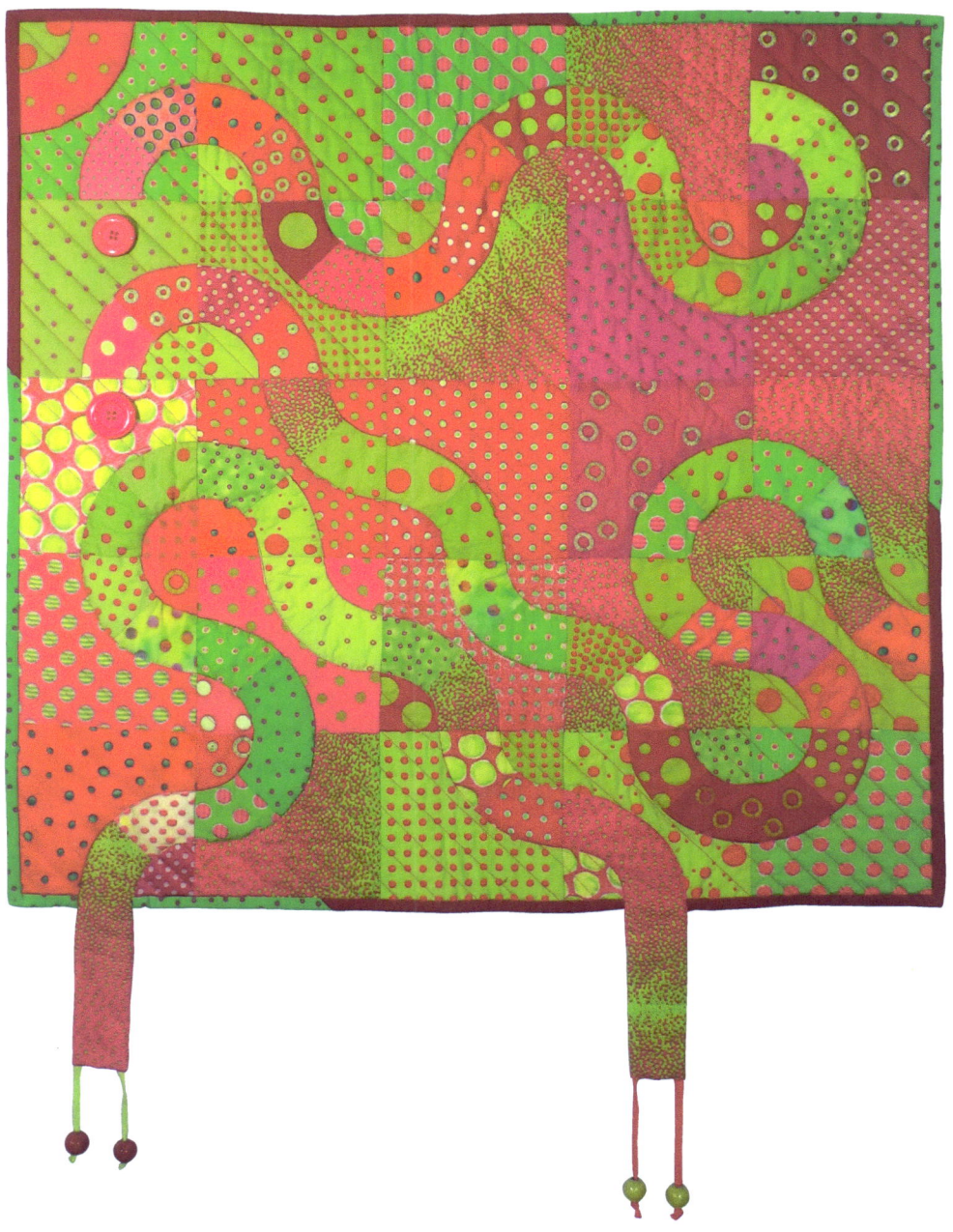

Convergence One: Cerise & Chartreuse, 2003-2011. 38˝ x 38˝, plus 14˝ extension.
Quilted and bound by Dani Lawler.

The quilt was nearly completed in 2003 when I was called away by other projects. When I refocused on quilting in 2011, my mind was a frenzy of designs, but my arthritis had advanced to where I could sew for only an hour or so a day and that with little pleasure.

Fortunately, I found two highly skilled Bay Area quilters, Dani Lawler and Katrina Lamken, who agreed to become my "constructionists." I would cut and arrange the fabric pieces on a large sheet of pattern paper. They would then photograph the pin-up to memorialize the design, roll up the paper and take it away to assemble and quilt. I then did the final embellishing. For *Convergence One*, constructionist Dani Lawler finished the machine quilting I had started in 2003 and did the binding. I then added the buttons and balls.

This quilt and Jane Sassaman's dot fabrics inspired three more ombréd two-color quilts, resulting in a series of four. Again, as I was putting away the many leftover cut-out pattern pieces, I found they weren't through with me yet. They soon became "babies," small versions of their "mother" quilts. Dating after the already-completed *Black Box* series (see page 44), these quilts continued letting the wandering arcs escape the rectangle of the quilt on the sides and tops, in addition to spilling out the bottom as in my first nine dot quilts. The eight small baby quilts are the culmination of that jail break.

Gemini, 2012. 25″ x 25″.
Constructed by Katrina Lamken.

Ouroboros, 2012. 25″ x 25″.
Constructed by Katrina Lamken.

Jane Sassaman's ombréd dots also inspired this cerulean and wheat color combo for *Convergence Two* and its babies. Additionally, I found commercial fabrics with blue-and-white or yellow-and-white dots, and colored in the white with fabric markers in the opposing color. Again, I did not have enough variety. Finally, I decided to design additional dots and have them custom printed. Graphic artist Ann Marra turned my rough sketches of various dot configurations into digital files, four different "fat quarters" to each yard, and I had them printed by Spoonflower (www.spoonflower.com) on their 42˝ wide basic combed cotton, plus a few dot patterns on their 54˝ wide cotton sateen. (See APPENDIX B: Resources.)

Convergence Two: Cerulean & Wheat, 2011. 38˝ x 37.5˝, plus 14˝ extension.
Constructed by Dani Lawler.

Crop Circles, 2011. 24˝ x 23.5˝.
Constructed by Dani Lawler.

Smoke Rings, 2011. 25˝ x 24˝.
Constructed by Dani Lawler.

Yet another Jane Sassaman ombréd color combination inspired *Convergence Three: Curry and Mauve*. And again, I designed additional dot combinations and had them custom printed by Spoonflower.

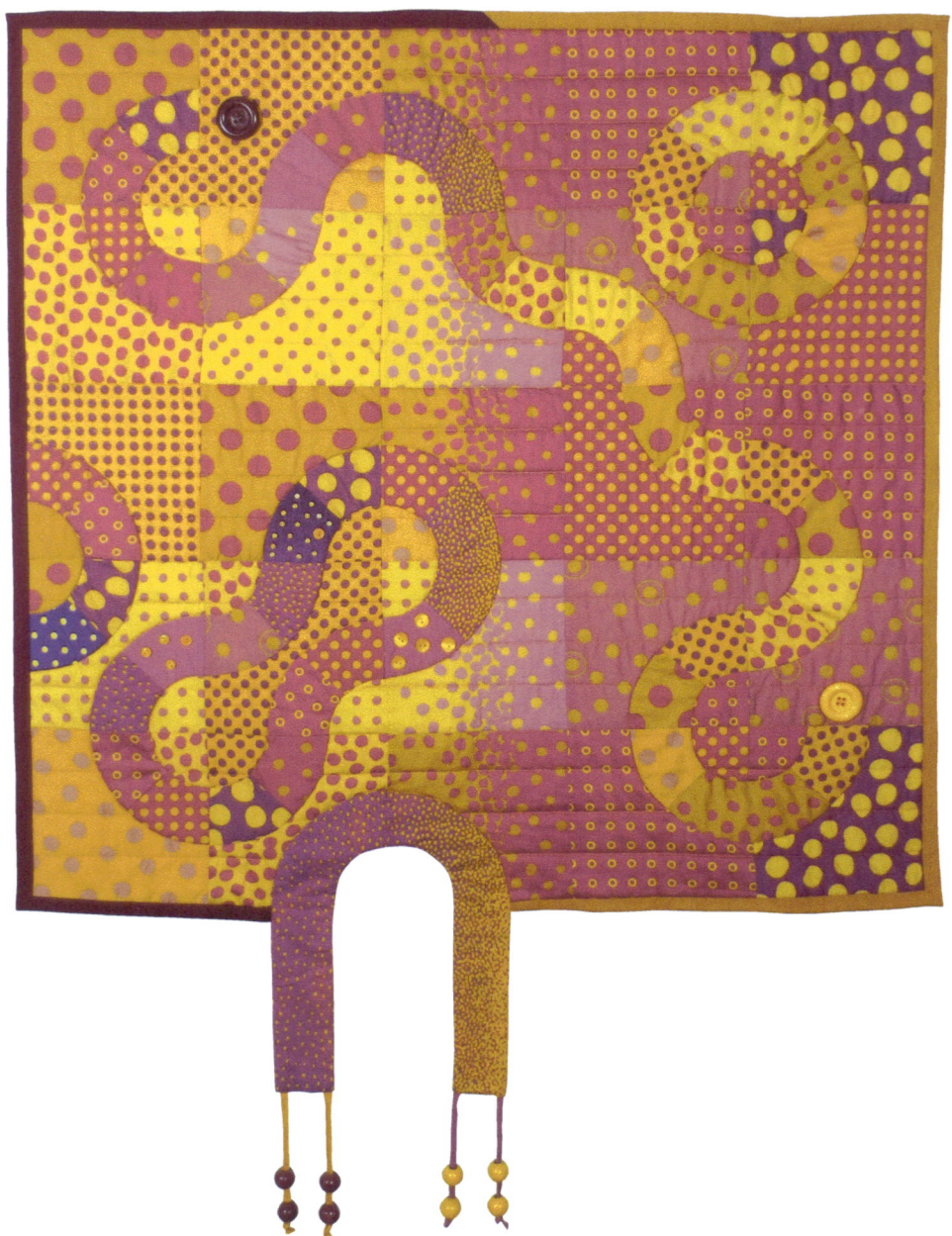

Convergence Three: Curry & Mauve, 2011. 39˝ x 39˝, plus 14˝ extension.
Constructed by Katrina Lamken.

Power Ball, 2011. 20˝ x 24˝.
Constructed by Dani Lawler.

Ball Park, 2011. 20˝ x 15˝.
Constructed by Dani Lawler.

Alas, no Jane Sassaman dots were issued in this, my favorite color combination, so I custom printed most of the fabrics for *Convergence Four: Teal & Terracotta*. I had sought the shimmery look of a fine Persian carpet, but the result seemed rather flat. I improvised with some brighter solids and embellishment to enrich the look.

Convergence Four: Teal & Terracotta, 2011. 38˝ x 38˝, plus 13˝ extension.
Constructed by Katrina Lamken.

Button Button, 2011. 20˝ x 20˝.
Constructed by Dani Lawler.

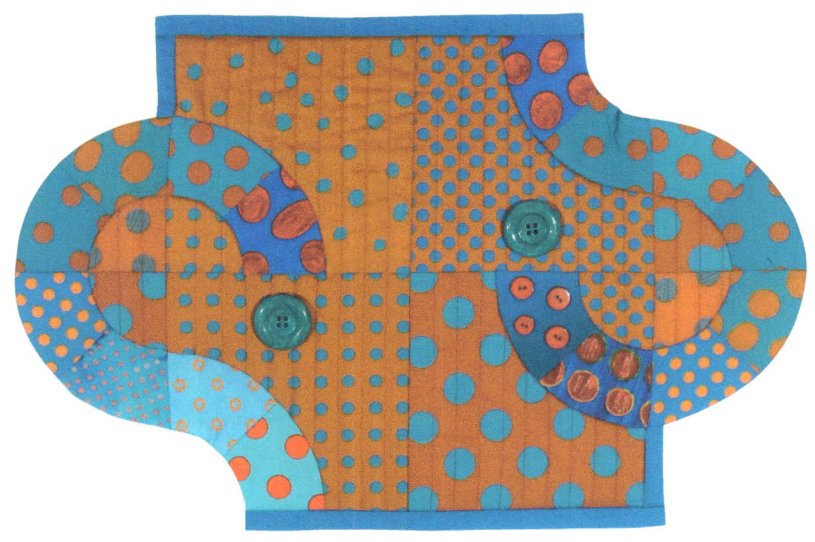

Who's Got the Button?, 2011. x 24˝ x 16˝.
Constructed by Dani Lawler.

The four large *Convergence* series quilts were off being assembled, and I was waiting for the first ones to start returning for embellishment. In this sudden lull after a frenzy of creativity, I spotted one of my favorite fabrics, a length of black polished cotton that I bought 25 years ago when quilt artist Sonia Lee Barrington had a stash sale. (It's not made anymore!) I began playing with the hundreds of dot fabrics I had collected and arranged in rainbow order in plastic bins. The *Black Box* series was the result. I also began thinking "outside the box" more aggressively, letting the wandering lines escape the frame of the quilt body on the sides and top as well as spilling out downward from the bottom. (The *Convergence* baby quilts, teamed for convenience with their parent quilt on previous pages, use this technique, but were actually made later.)

Black Box: Red, 2011. 32˝ x 32˝.
Constructed by Dani Lawler.

Black Box: Indigo, 2011. 23.5˝ x 31.5˝.
Constructed by Dani Lawler.

Black Box: Green, 2011. 27.5˝ x 27.5˝.
Constructed by Dani Lawler.

(When Dani bound *Black Box: Green*, she matched the top half of a white dot on the navy fabric with the bottom half of a white dot in the navy arc running into the binding. I love it!)

Black Box: White, 2011. 31.5˝ x 27.5˝.
Constructed by Dani Lawler.

Black Box: Yellow, 2011. 31.5˝ x 31.5˝.
Constructed by Dani Lawler.

In sorting my dots by color, I discovered that I had accumulated two large boxes of red-and-white dots, though I had never used this combo. Some were gifts from people who knew I was the "dot" person and so had brought me their scraps, dumpster finds, and cast-offs. These red-and-white fabrics begged to become a pair of large quilts, ultimately *Confetti I* and *Confetti II*, and then their offspring.

Confetti I, 2011. 52˝ x 41˝.
Constructed by Katrina Lamken.

Confetti II, 2011. 49˝ x 44˝.
Constructed by Katrina Lamken.

Subsequently, the *Confetti* quilts mated and produced a pair of "babies."

Streamers: Red, 2011. 25˝ x 25˝.
Constructed by Dani Lawler.

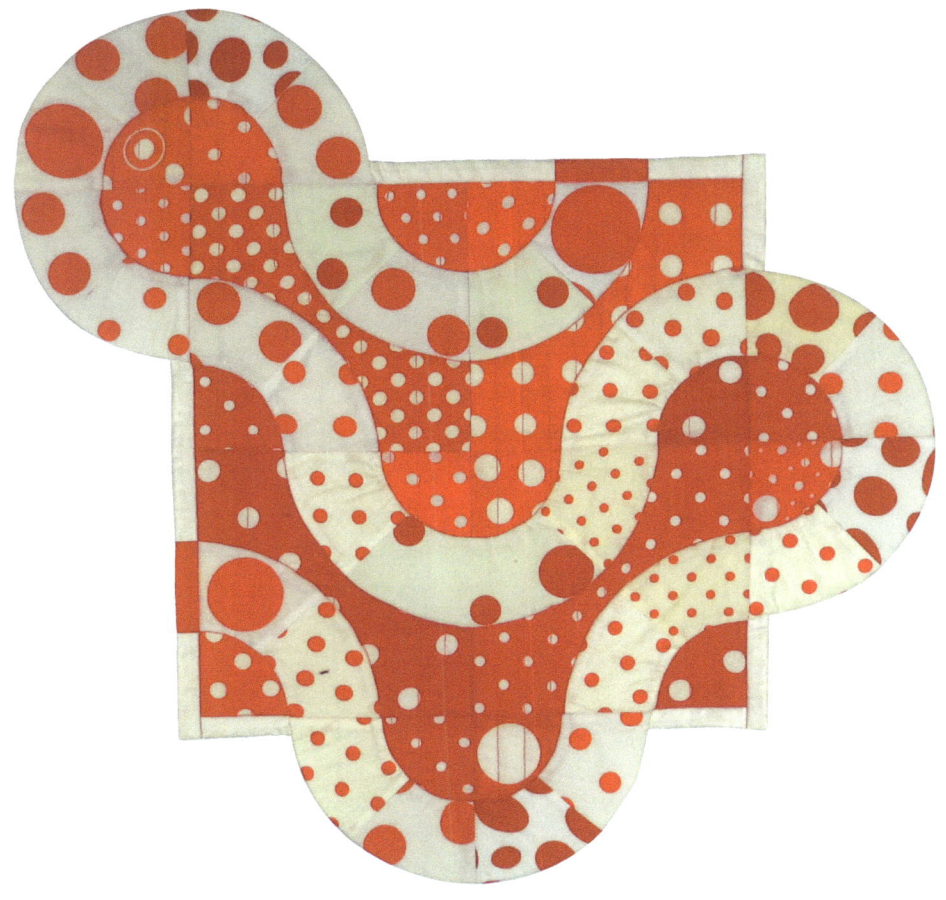

Streamers: White, 2011. 24˝ x 24˝.
Constructed by Dani Lawler.

Tiny Bubbles represents a diversion from all-dots. I have always adored Hawaiian fabrics and wanted to see if I could morph them into each other, with a sparkling river running through. I had nearly finished this piece in 2005 when I was distracted by other projects. When I returned to it in 2011, I decided to use Katie Pasquini's ombréd dots for the water. For embellishment, to create the absolutely perfect bubbles I tried to locate the lightweight, opalescent plastic cabochons that I recall using by the great gross for *The King and I* costumes in the 1960s. Sadly, it seems they are no longer made. I substituted heavy (and expensive) glass beads to twinkle on the water's path. Bead fringes tumble as mini waterfalls.

Tiny Bubbles, 2005-2011. 32˝ x 46˝, plus 12˝ extensions and beaded fringe.
Quilting and binding completed by Dani Lawler in 2011.

Meander kicked off a new mini-series of tall quilts for lofty spaces. It was inspired by and made especially for showings of my quilts in several places with 30-feet-plus ceilings.

The back of Meander is also a design unto itself.

Meander, 2012. 54˝ x 39.5˝.
Constructed by Dani Lawler.

This triptych depicts seaweed rising from the bottom of the ocean, up from darkness toward sunlight. When it was completed, I held my breath to see if it would hang straight or go all cattywampus. It hangs straight.

Seaweed, 2012. 101″ x 50″.
Constructed by Dani Lawler.

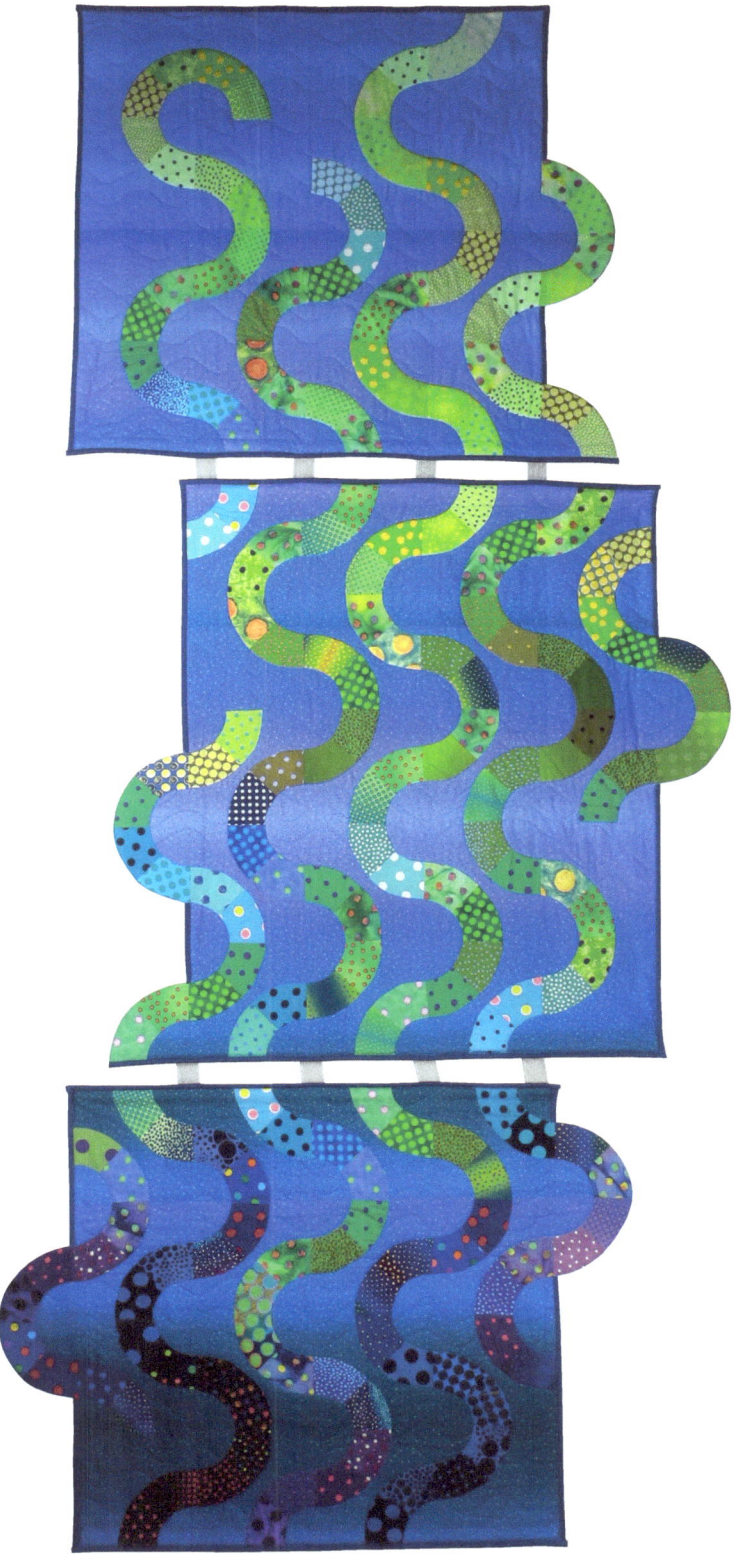

An experiment with using my basic block "on point" (diagonal) for the first time. This let me move arcs outside the central space in a way that, to me, represented plunging water and spray. The open spaces created by the top arcs require a Plexiglass® backing to help the arcs to stand up straight. The Plexiglass® also substitutes for the usual hanging bar.

Waterfall, 2012. 90″ x 38″.
Constructed by Katrina Lamken.

Bonfire is red flames rising, a logical companion to *Waterfall*, which is blue water descending. Again, a Plexiglass® structure is used to support the top and hang the piece.

Bonfire, 2013. 97″ x 41″.
Constructed by Dani Lawler.

Low-tech Dots

Not all quilters have access to high-tech computerized printers and sewing machines to create custom dot fabric. Here are some low-tech ways to produce unusual color combinations of dots for your projects.

- Overdye commercial fabrics. If you're not sure of potential results, check a color wheel or do a small sample to see what happens if you dye blue over yellow, etc. Also, different fibers take dye differently.
- Buy fabric with one of your two desired colors as background plus white polka dots. Color in the dots with a permanent fabric pen in your other color.
- Block print dots, using fabric paints. Create printing blocks by carving patterns on linoleum blocks (available at art stores) or any firm media like a potato. Or use round objects like corks. Apply paint to the block surface using a breyer (little roller) or smear paint in a flat disposable dish and dip the block, blotting off excess on a paper towel. Keep your eyes open for things like building supplies and packing materials that can transfer a dot pattern to fabric. Remember that donut shapes are also circles. Use tiny jar tops, kitchen articles, or cut-off sections of pipe. Dip them in fabric paint and dot your fabric.
- Rub on dots. Place round objects—coins, poker chips, washers, etc.—under tightly stretched cloth and rub with fabric crayons. Fix according to manufacturer's directions.
- Make freezer paper stencils. Cut or punch dots in the paper. Iron onto fabric and paint with opaque fabric paints. Caution: Dried paint on used stencils might damage your iron, so clean stencils carefully before reusing. If possible, prepare several freezer-paper stencils at one time by ironing squares of paper together in a stack before punching. Leather and scrapbooking punches are good tools for a variety of hole sizes.
- Fuse dots. Affix two-faced fusible to the back of the material you want to be dots. Then cut dots from it with leather or scrap-booking punches or with scissors. Fuse to background fabric with a hot iron, following manufacturer's directions. Large dots should then be secured to your background fabric by sewing around the dot with zigzag machine stitch or by hand with a blanket stitch. Overstitch small dots with invisible thread so they don't pop off.
- Use buttons, especially jumbo coat buttons and tiny doll buttons, for a variety of dots.
- Sew donut-dots on your sewing machine without special attachments. Push a carpet tack or thumb tack through the sticky side of painters' or masking tape. Tape to the bed of your sewing machine about an inch to the left of the needle so the sharp tack point sticks up. Place a square of background on the tack point and secure with a cork. Lower feed dogs and sew with zigzag stitch, using dot color thread, cotton or rayon. You can thus combine any two colors in one dotted fabric.

Embellishments

The world is full of round things, many of which yearn to become polka dots on fiber art pieces. The most logical ones are buttons, but consider also items found at hardware, stationery, and grocery stores, floral supplies, electronic and computer parts, broken jewelry, industrial discards found at recycling centers. When you walk down the street or enter a store with dots in mind, an amazing number of objects appear.

Also:

LACE: Consider cut-out round segments from machine or handmade lace, using contemporary yardage from bridal shops or old pieces from thrift shops. This is a good way to recycle lace and crochet work too tattered for other uses.

CROCHET: Create circles and donut-shapes by crocheting yarn, string, or metallic cords. If you're not an experienced crocheter, follow the standard instructions for starting an afghan block, chaining, joining, and then crocheting one round of stitches. Stop and secure end of yarn.

COGS, JEWELRY BITS, ELECTRONIC PARTS, BOTTLE TOPS: Sew an ordinary shank button to your piece, then glue decorative item directly to the button. Use hot glue. Or, if practical and artistically pleasing, drill tiny holes in the item itself and sew the item on as you would a regular button.

WASHERS: Attach donut-shaped items to the surface by stitching over them in several places to secure them, or cover them entirely with colored thread.

APPENDIX A

About the Block

> There is a story of a Zen master presenting a student with a goldfish in a bowl and instructing him to study and draw the fish. The student does so for an hour, then brings the drawings to the master. "No," the master says gently, "I said to study and draw the fish." The student continues for many years and never exhausts new discoveries.

It doesn't matter which block excites your interest. I encourage you to find one or create one and then see how far you can push it. Maybe you'll exhaust all possibilities with a few quilts. More likely, as with the Zen student, you'll find yourself going down a road with infinite potential for exploration and discovery.

In my case, I have concentrated on a variation of a traditional American quilt block that goes by several names. The basic block has two pieces and looks as if you could cut a quarter circle from the corner of two squares, swap the pie-segment pieces, and sew each block into a new block. Of course, this isn't possible because it leaves out the necessary seam allowance.

Basic "Borrow from Peter to Pay Paul" block

Because curved seaming scares a lot of sewers, various methods have been devised to avoid it. However, because of my strong dressmaking background, curves never phased me. They are surprisingly easy, so if your chosen pattern contains them, give them a try. Only after quilt #29 did I try adding the arcs separately on top of a finished square by appliqué.

APPENDIX B

Resources

Supplies

Dharma Trading Co • www.dharmatrading.com. 1805 S. McDowell Blvd. Ext., Petaluma, CA 94954. (800) 542-5227. 8-5 PST, M-F. An excellent source of dyes, fabric markers, and transfer supplies.

Spoonflower • www.spoonflower.com. One of various on-line services that lets you create your own fabric by submitting digital files. They print in sizes from 8˝ x 8˝ swatches up to a single design covering several yards. While you will need to deal with them by computer to upload your files, you can also phone them at (919) 886-7885.

Bibliography

Cory, Pepper, *Happy Trails, Variations on the Classic Drunkard's Path*, 1991. C&T Publishing, Lafayette, California. Excellent history and chronicle of variations of the block I used in this series. I didn't discover this book until 2013!

Mashuta, Mary, *Confetti Quilts: A No-Fuss Approach to Color, Fabric & Design*, 2003, C&T Publishing, Lafayette, California. Includes instructions for use of her Circle within a Circle block.

APPENDIX C

My Life in Rags
From Costumes to Quilts

Originally published in *SF Art Forum*, June 1986

Lots of people laugh. "Why," they ask, "do you take a big piece of cloth, cut it up into little pieces, and then sew them back into big pieces again?"

It's a reasonable question. The art and craft of quilting has progressed from a survival skill of the struggling to a pastime for the leisured and even, occasionally, an art form. Why do we still resort to the meticulous piecework developed by our forebearers back when a yard of machine-woven cloth cost a week's wages, and every scrap had to be used?

Today's quilters have almost unlimited fabrics and fibers to work with, but we still insist on reducing the whole to smaller elements, then reconstructing our personal vision of color, texture, and density. You might as well ask painters why they open their paint tubes when the colors are already so neatly sorted out. Or ask masons or carpenters why they break up one whole to create another. It is essential to creativity, a basic human need to alter our environment on a large or small scale.

I came to quilting after many years as a stage costumer, accustomed to combining a myriad of fabrics, colors, and textures into a whole. A stage costume has some advantages over a quilt as a work of art. It is literally stage center in the spotlight, demanding attention, powerfully supported by the drama of the moment and the movement and actions of the wearer. It has context and immediacy.

Designing a stage costume is a collaboration, rather like being an architect. The design must fit in the whole production and allow for such things as quick changes, body mikes, and choreography. It must please both the director and the actor—and often extraneous bystanders. Even when budgets are large enough to cover fine materials and skilled construction people, costumes are always built on ridiculously tight schedules. The designer walks a perilous course between integrity, expediency, and compromise until the finished costume appears before an audience. Costumes are a fugitive art. Like the performance they support, they are specific to a moment and age rapidly, rarely surviving more than a few months, sometimes only a few weeks, before they must be replaced.

When I turned from costuming to child raising, I decided that quilting might offer an even more satisfying medium—a chance to be absolute boss, to control all the elements of design without the frustration of collaboration. The intense tactile satisfaction of working with fabric is the same, the almost sinful fulfillment of soft, rough, smooth against the fingers.

There's the delight of collecting and combining the mundane and the tasteless—the polyester daisy print, some white-on-white shirting, pajama flannel, op and pop and slop art fabrics—with fragments of your own clothing. As with Prospero's "sea change," the tiny bits become "something rich and strange," losing their identities as they mutate into a glowing and subtle tapestry.

Yet there are drawbacks to quilting too. Compared to the union wages of a costumer, a quilter's income (if she can bear to sell anything) is diddlysquat. Fibers are still fragile. Few quilts survive beyond their owner's lifetime, and then rarely another hundred years. Quilting is still considered a craft, not an art. Interest in quilts is cyclical, like hula hoops and canasta. Decorator magazines routinely show old quilts lying on floors or used as tablecloths on picnic tables heavy with juicy watermelon slices and dripping barbecue. Even wall quilts by recognized artists are really just commercial art. They are bought with a preordained percentage of the corporate budget and used to "humanize" a blank office space until soil, fluorescent lighting, and neglect take their toll.

My first quilts went on beds, where quilts are supposed to go, a logical extension of the sensuality of the creative process. Puppies' claws, upset tummys, and Hawaiian Punch quickly aged them into retirement. The wall was my next site, remote from many daily disasters, but also from the direct contact that makes fabric so personal. But, I comforted myself, tapestries and carpets evolved to cover walls, to keep out the cold while providing warmth for the eye and the spirit.

I sort my colors. Somewhere in the pile may be just the right gray-green to support one end of the amber bar as it emerges from the field of plum and gray diamonds. Helpful friends look at my latest effort and ask, "Where are you going to hang it?" There is nowhere to put it. It exists, not to fill a space on my wall, but a space in my heart.

They say encouragingly, "Why don't you make a Gone with the Wind quilt?" or "a Wizard of Oz quilt?" I smile and nod and go back to my triangles and parallelograms. Speak to me rather of 72-degree angles and Wang dominoes, of nonrepeating tessellations. My palette and patterns are nearly limitless, my inspiration extended by computer graphics, my medium as old as the first creature who gathered vines to use as ropes. I have moved my rags from the spotlight to a private place where few others look with my eyes. But the vision is all mine.

Alphabetical List of Quilts

Ball One	25
Ball Park	41
Black Box: Green	47
Black Box: Indigo	46
Black Box: Red	45
Black Box: White	48
Black Box: Yellow	49
Bonfire	63
Button Button	43
Confetti I	50
Confetti II	51
Convergence Four: Teal & Terracotta	42
Convergence One: Cerise & Chartreuse	33
Convergence Three: Curry & Mauve	40
Convergence Two: Cerulean & Wheat	37
Crop Circles	38
Dot-Dot-Dot	29
Gemini	35
Going Dotty I	30
Going Dotty II	31
Hot Spot	23
Meander	57
Night Spot	28
Ouroboros	25
Power Ball	41
Seaweed	59
Smoke Rings	39
Streamers: Red	52
Streamers: White	53
Sun Spot	27
Tiny Bubbles	55
Waterfall	61
Who's Got the Button?	43

Eleanor Knowles Dugan is an avid writer, researcher, and quilter. She has written or edited thirty books on business, communications, and film topics, plus more than fifty articles about quilts and quilters for publications including *Quilters Newsletter* magazine, *Quilting Quarterly*, *The Quilter*, *Women's Day*, and *Lady's Patchwork Circle*. In 2007, she presented a paper before the American Quilt Study Group. She turned to quilting in the early 1970s after twenty years as a costume designer in New York and Los Angeles.

www.EleanorDuganQuilts.com.

Katrina Lamken has been quilting for over 20 years and is a member of the San Francisco Quilters Guild. She makes traditional and art quilts, as well as wearable art. She is well versed in hand and machine piecing, appliqué, and hand and machine quilting. Katrina teaches quilting classes in the Bay Area and has taught at Black Cat Quilts in San Francisco for many years. Her quilts and wearables have been exhibited at local and national shows. She has a BA from San Francisco State University in Design and Industry.

Dani Lawler completed her first quilt in 1969. Unfortunately, it disintegrated in its first washing. Subsequent quilts have survived, many shown at the San Francisco Quilters Guild biennial quilt shows where she placed first in Wearable Art in 2011. She has also exhibited at the Sanchez Art Center and the Pacific International Quilt Festival, Northern California Quilt Council section.

*Glory be to God for dappled things—
For skies of couple-colour as a brinded cow;
For rose-moles all in stipple upon trout that swim;
Fresh-firecoal chestnut falls; finches' wings;
…Whatever is fickle, freckled (who knows how?)….*

              Gerald Manley Hopkins, 1918

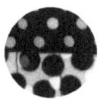